First Printing, 2018
Wild Cabbage Books
wildcabbagebooks.com

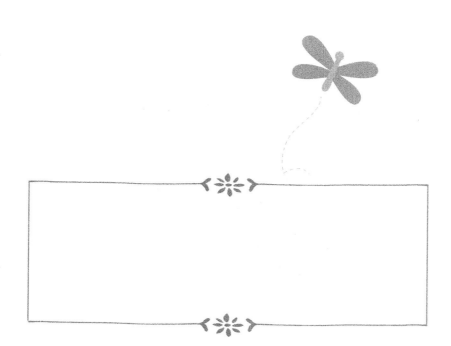

Each of us is limitless; each of us with his or her right upon the earth.

– Walt Whitman

> This above all: to thine ownself be true.
>
> – Shakespeare

Excellence is not an act, but a habit.

– Aristotle

No act of kindness, no matter how small, is ever wasted.
— Aesop

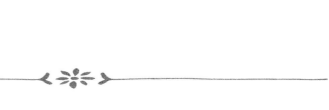

The way to be happy is to make others so.

— Robert Ingersoll

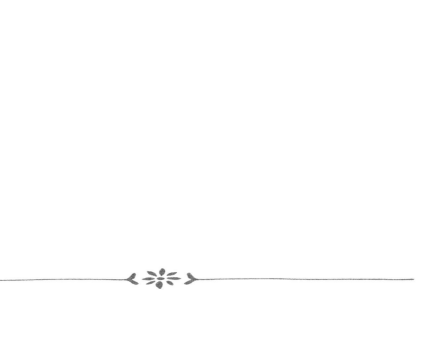

Be happy for this moment. This moment is your life.

– Omar Kayyam

Peace is always beautiful.

— Walt Whitman

The greatest mistake you can make in life is to be continually fearing you will make one.

— Elbert Hubbard

Bloom where you are planted.

— 1 Corinthians KJV

Made in the
USA
Middletown, DE